Root cause

A real world guide to stopping disasters happening ever again

By

DAVID BUXTON

Introduction

There is a truth that I'd like to share with you, almost every company and business, big or small has from time to time issues, problems and disasters. That's not big news I hear you say and you'd be right. What might suprise you though is, almost all of these companies don't know how to stop these issues, problems and disasters from happening again and again. Sure they know what root cause is and in the larger companies have staff trained to find and eliminate what they think is the root cause. Problem is the issues keep coming back again and again! The reason they keep coming back again and again is simple, the way most text books and companies train their staff has more chance of finding Lord Lucan, riding Shergar with this week's lottery numbers in his pocket, than they do of finding a true root cause outside of the classroom.

This book is a real world, step by step guide to stopping any type of undesirable event from ever happening ever again.

It will show you how to investigate any issue/problem/disaster and then how to discover and eliminate the trigger that starts the undesirable chain of events. Making it imposible to ever happen again.

Index

Something went horribly and inextricably wrong! After going through such a horrible experience, you need to make damn sure it won't come back.

You don't need a sticking plaster, let's see how that bodge goes, type of fix, but a permanent, cast iron, guaranteed, 100% it won't ever happen again fix.

We have all been through tough times, break-ups. Accidents and failures to name just a few of the horrible experiences we all have been through. If that event did or very nearly wrecked your business, health, relationship, happiness or financial stability etc. the last thing you would want is for it to happen again and again. After all, what's to stop it?

The only way to guarantee any problem will never, ever return is to find where the problem began and what triggered the chain of events that lead to the issue/problem/disaster. We call this original trigger point the root cause.

This book will guide you practically through a simple, tried and tested, straightforward, 7-step method to finding the root cause of any issue, problem or disaster. It doesn't matter if this issue is in your home, in your business or on an international scale. This method works on all scales and in all situations.

Don't worry if you or others have previously tried to put it right, and it just keeps coming back, or if it's the first time anyone has seen this difficulty. This book will show and guide you through the steps to finding the true root cause and then how to stop it happening ever again.

The size of the issue is significant to you or to your company, but this practical method works on all issues regardless of their size, cost, or importance.

It could be that the issue nearly killed you or very nearly brought your whole company down. So, you really can't risk a repeat. On the other hand, it might be like a leaking tap. It's not the end of the world, it's just annoying and money and profits are slowly and constantly flowing down the drain.

This book will help you to stop the most serious or the day-to-day concerns forever.

It's obvious that issues are best resolved quickly, but don't worry whether you've inherited an old problem, or you've been super busy and only just found time to get around to sorting this little niggle out. This system still works long after the event. So, never think it's too late.

This book will explain and guide you step by step, not through the theory that only works in a classroom, but with real-world theory that truly works.

Let's get straight into stopping that unwanted event ever happening again.

How far can I go back and still find a root cause?

The more time that passes, the greater chance the evidence has become polluted or difficult to obtain? Armed with this knowledge, you will have to understand the extra effort needed to correct an issue/problem/disaster. .

That's not to say it's not worth going back 5 years or even 25 years as long as there is enough evidence to work with. My advice with older   is Just to be realistic.

As we said, there is no limit to how far you can go back, as long as you're realistic and don't use assumptions or guesses to fill in the investigation's gaps..

Chapter 2

Theory books suggested methods for root cause

Let's begin by taking a look at the methods most theory books suggest will find an issue/problem/disaster's root cause;

These are the methods used in industry worldwide, with billions to be lost off from big disasters you would think they would be real slick....

First up it's

BRAINSTORMING

This is a middle manager's favorite. Basically, it's a crowd guessing game. No matter how many people there are in the room and no matter how smart and experienced they all are. They are all guessing. How do we know this? Because in almost every case, there has not been a structured investigation before the brainstorming session.

So, why do companies and especially middle managers love this method? To begin with, it's quick and requires minimum effort to arrange. The method uses staff already managed by the department, (so no additional cost or budget adjustment is required). Additional middle manager's jump at this method because they can be seen to have quickly taken action, (this is important to the middle manager because the big boss will asks him or her in the next management meeting, in front of the other middle managers, what they are doing about the disaster?)

Brainstorming sessions, gives them an instant answer, (the other managers all take note that this is a good method to keep the boss happy at minimal cost and effort). A second reason it's a middle manager preferred method is, that it's super easy to use the brainstorming session to give out additional tasks, again if asked they've now got a working plan that's being actioned by a team. Doesn't that sound great?

Basically, for minimum effort, the middle manager looks like they are being proactive and things are all under control.

Why doesn't this extremely popular method work?

To begin with, people who have axes to grind can use the meeting to air their grievances and point fingers, (this includes the manager). Most if not all the people in the meeting will only have knowledge of the section of the process they work on.

IN OTHER WORDS, NO ONE CAN SEE THE WHOLE PICTURE!

Of course most of the people in the meeting will be experts at their section of the process, so it's most likely the meeting will get bogged down in detail. A situation the manager will be happy about because he can give out tasks to meddle with the detail. The manager, if he or she has anything about them, will now steer the meeting any which way they choose. This invariably means for their own career/office politics interest.

I'll say this again and again, from a root cause perspective, brainstorming is a complete and utter waste of everyone's time.

The law of averages says that if you guess enough times once in a blue moon, you'll be correct. This is the only hope you have using this method, blind luck.

Just think of what all of those highly skilled, well-paid staff could/should have been doing! Certainly, they are not working making profits because I promise you that brainstorming will not permanently resolve the problem. So, when everyone is looking for a pay rise next year, think back over the past year and remember how much company money has been wasted in meetings like this.

FISHBONE diagram or ISIKOWA diagram

Next up is the second most used root cause method, a FISHBONE or ISIKOWA diagram

Two different names, but they are one and the same thing (and also both produce the same poor result). Yet again, all this method is good for is to justify that middle management have done something.

Allow me to explain how these meetings usually pan out;

So that something is seen to being done and just in case their boss quizzes the middle manager in their next meeting. The manager hastily gathers a selection of the department's staff into a meeting room. Here, they all discuss as many of the undesirable events EFFECTS that they can all think of. They then pop all these effects onto the fish bone/Isikowa diagram. Next they all stand back, suck their teeth and decide the root cause has to be where the most effects appear.

The next chapter (Chapter 3) explains the difference between effect and cause.

The manager now puts his/her spin on what they are looking at, (he/she won't want their department being the problem, as that could adversely affect his/her budget and carrier prospects).

From a root cause perspective, when you see a fish bone/Isikowa diagram, just know it's worse than a complete waste of everybody's time. It's a distraction. And worse than the brainstorming guessing game, as there is no slight chance that this method will yield anything apart from a happy middle manager.

FAULT TREE ANALYSIS

The next method (less often used than BRAINSTORMING and FISHBONE). Is called a FAULT TREE ANALYSIS, this is basically a fish bone diagram turned on it's side, as you might have guessed they're of little use when it comes to root cause. As discussed previously, it is actually counterproductive as it sends everyone off chasing effects. If you're called into a meeting, and they start using this method (or the fishbone/Isikowa), be aware that you're not going to find the root cause and your manager, when it comes to root cause, doesn't know what they are doing. (Or they are using the problem to forward their own career interests).

5Y's (five whys)

To find a root cause this is the only method, in conjunction with a structured investigation that will find the true root cause, repeatedly and reliably.

Please be aware that as good as this method is, IT CANNOT, find the root cause on its own. There has to be a structured investigation carried out before the 5Ys and by the same person.

Because this is the only method that works out in real-world situations, we will look at this method in detail, along with real-world examples, all in its own chapter. (Chapter 5).

Chapter 3

The difference between effect and cause, (root cause in our case).

We have talked a lot in the previous chapter about the EFFECTS of an issue/problem/disaster. As this is where most people get their directions mixed up and when you're actually checking something easy to forget, let's take a look at the difference between cause and effect in relation to finding an issue's root cause.

Understanding the subtle difference is the key to success when it comes to finding the true root cause.

So let's dive in, put simply, an EFFECT is just what it sounds as if it's going to be:

Any unplanned action resulting from the issue/problem/disaster.

Whereas a CAUSE is the point in the process where the unplanned effect came from.

The reason it's important to be totally aware about the difference between the two is because this is where many people, businesses, and even governments make a simple mistake, confusing the two. This in turn means they will never find the root cause. They mistake effect for cause. What typically happens is they see only the effects and try to put fixes in place for them. (fire fighting, in other words). Or worse still, they try to see a pattern in the effects and waste their time on something they think is causing their collection of effects. (guessing, in other words).

In general, the root cause is not what can obviously be seen going wrong. You have to dig deeper.

Let's look at a couple of examples of the difference between effect and cause.

The titanic sank—effect

She sank because she was going too fast in the dark to avoid the iceberg—cause.

Ah, I can hear you saying. When the great liner hit the gigantic iceberg, didn't it slit the Hull open? Isn't that the cause? Hitting the ice burg is an effect, as is the Hull being opened up to allow the sea in.

To clarify an effect is something that happened BECAUSE of the incident.

Whereas a cause is part of the STANDARD operation or process.

Looking at the Titanic example, the actions of sinking, filling with water, hitting the iceberg, opening the Hull etc. all happened BECAUSE of the incident; therefore they are all EFFECTS.

Whereas going at full speed in the dark was standard practice back in those days. (a new liner on a maiden voyage needed to break records and generate publicity).

Let's look at another disaster closer to home that many of us have had to face, a relationship break up.

Let's imagine that Susan's partner has left her and gone to live her best friend.

Both leaving and going to live with her now ex best friend are both EFFECTS.

Let's say Susan's ex partner is a serial cheater and had left another girl to be with Susan. We could then say that is a CAUSE. It is the ex-partner's standard practice!

Try to think about issues in your life or on the news and practice spotting what is an EFFECT (happening because of the event) and what is a CAUSE (the point in the standard operation where things went wrong).

The reason we are spending so much time on this is because when you're looking at an issue it's easy to forget and mix the two up. (watch the news, and you'll see politicians, government's and big company's doing it all the time).

Let's start with a nice, simple scenario for you to practice your new-found skill on ;

(We will then move on to a couple of commonly found scenarios again to give you practice).

Scenario 1

Let's begin with someone called Fred who has a bicycle with a puncture.

The tire has little or no air in it and the bike is unrideable. Are these effect or causes?

When Fred goes to mend his bike, he finds there's a hole in the inner tube, where the air has escaped from. Is this a cause or effect?

When Fred investigates further, he finds he has ridden over a big thorn which has gone through the tire into the inner tube? Is this thorn a cause or an effect? Looking at the thorn, Fred remembers he has ridden down a lane where the Hawthorn hedge has recently been cut. Is this a cause or an effect?

The answers to the questions are:

Puncture.

No air in tire.

Hole in inner tube?

Hole in tire

Thorn.

Are all effects.

Ridding down the lane

cutting the thorn hedge

are causes, did you spot them easily? If you did, well done, but if you didn't, just go back for a second and read it again. While bearing in mind what is a normal operation.

In this scenario, no matter how many times Fred repairs the puncture, i.e., spends time and effort on the effect(s) until he stops riding where the thorns are (cause) the problem of flat tires will continue.

Note; It's much more economical in time and cash to use a little resource and effort to find the root cause, than it is to keep fixing the effects over and over again.

Let's look at a second scenario:

Sally has a picture framing business, but she has an issue, the precut glass her supplier has sent to her won't fit in her frames. (is this is an effect or a cause)? She has checked, and the glass is correct, however when she checked the frames she had made herself, she found that her frames are coming out the wrong size. (is this a cause or an effect)? Sally uses a jig to make her frames, so she double-checked the jig and discovered that the measurement scale for the frames' width is out of position. (is this a cause or an effect)? Thinking back, she remembers dropping the jig (an effect or a cause)? At the time, she redecorated the shop. She had tried to move it on her own instead of waiting for some help.

The glass not fitting.

The frames incorrect size.

The jigs scale

dropping the jig.

Are all effects

of moving the jig for decorating,

is a cause.

Example 3

Your company has just had an external audit which found a few small minor findings and unfortunately one serious major finding that threatens to take away the companies' accreditation, which if removed, would result in the cancellation of present orders and a loss of future business.

The minor and major findings, the threat of losing the accreditation along with loosing present and future orders are all causes or effects?

The major audit finding was that the company had no internal audit plan and that the business had not carried out any internal or external audits for over three years.

So, what would you class as the effects of the issue, and what would you think was a cause?

The company receiving audit findings and the possible loss of customers and orders are all effects, whereas the companies' policy of not auditing and not having a plan are both causes.

I used this last example to show a cause can be something that is usually carried out or something that is usually not carried out, either way up to this point it's a standard process.

Chapter 4

The 7 step investigation

Step one

Define the problem

Defining the issue, problem or disaster, regardless of it scale, is done very simply by writing the problem down.

I would urge you to physically write it down using old-fashioned pen and paper (it's OK to also open a file on your chosen device).

Why am I urging you to physically write it down? There are three reasons why;

1. We need to be 100% clear what the issue is. (You would be amazed how, even some of the world's biggest and best thought of companies, don't really have a definitive answer when I ask them what the actual issue is? Even when they've hired me in to fix it!)

2. You need to be open-minded when looking for clues as you work towards the root cause. It's a well known psychological technique to physically write an issue down. The physical connection from your brain controlling your muscles to move the pen connects your brain via your arm, hand, and pen to the paper, this transfers the issue psychologically from your head to the paper. In this way, this technique stops your subconscious working away 24/7 on the issue. In our case, that helps keep your mind open.

3. It's important to be able to refer to the exact issue, especially if it's a large or complex issue that you're looking at. That point of reference can

be significant, (for reasons we'll discuss later in chapter 5) but crucially to help keep your investigation on the right track.

If you're in a business environment, a small pocket sized notebook is the best place to write the problem down in. (Small because it will discourage you from making numerous notes but still be convenient enough for you to take everywhere with you).

Note: if like many Engineers you use a daybook, keep your small root cause notebook separate and leave your daybook behind when you're investigating, (you really don't want to look like you're an auditor).

If you're doing this at home, again I again recommend a small pocket notebook but don't worry if you don't have one, it's not essential where you write it down. A sticky note on the fridge for instance, it's just essential that you write it down where you can find it easily again and refer to it. If you're in a business environment, in addition to writing the issue in your small pocket sized notebook, you'll also have to follow your business processes and enter the issue into your companies non conformance system. Again, it's important that you can keep referring back to the original problem. (If someone has made a hash of entering the issue at an earlier date, this is the time to get it resolved so that the company's system has the correct and definitive issue recorded).

Now you've finished step one, defining the issue. It's now time for you or your organisation to investigate the issue, so the second thing you need to do is identify a person to carry out the investigation. This is the next step towards finding the root cause.

Step two

Identify the investigator

If you're doing the investigation at home, or you're a one-person business/sole trader, then step two will be quicker and easier than step one was. It will be simple to see who will be carrying out the investigation—you!

However, if you're in a large business or work environment. Who should be chosen to carry out the investigation?

Let's look at why the vast majority of real-world businesses, set up their root cause investigations to fail from day one.

Why? Because they send a team in, instead of sending in the right person.

Yep, you read that right, the correct individual is certainly going to be more successful than a team.

What you're looking for in a root cause investigator is;

The person selected for the investigation has to be somebody who is familiar with the process and knows the process from end to end. What you absolutely don't need is a team of people. I've heard these teams called all sorts of silly names, dragon team, expert teams, RCI teams and all sorts of strange and wonderful names. Allow me to explain to you the reality of these teams. They will only distract each other, create more tasks and waste time. Crucially, they will never find the root cause, (more often as not they will report they found it. When in fact what they've found is an effect of the issue, not even a cause, and certainly not the issue's true root cause).

Let's look at what you really require for root cause success. Choose a single person, not a team, and certainly not a committee.

You just require a smart, open-minded person who is familiar with that type of process. It's also important that they are from another area of your business, that is independent of the area and process that has the issue. Again, if you're at home or a one-man business you won't have this luxury/problem, but on the other hand you'll be very familiar with the issue and the process. You or the person appointed to investigate absolutely need to be completely open-minded. That is, don't try to guess or begin with preconceived ideas. Of course, we are all human and will have a hunch or that nagging thought about something, but for now, you must put this away. (It will come in useful later, but for now, bury it deep down, so it can't influence you in any way). Start with a mental clean sheet.

That's all you need. No big team. No drama and no song and dance, where managers play office politics with other departments/managers or use the investigation to improve their career options.

Allow me to explain why I'm putting a lot of emphasis on this. Plenty of companies think like this;

Big problem = big team.

Big losses = spend lots to correct.

What's wrong with big teams tackling issues? After all, isn't team work what a business is all about?

In many situation's teamwork is a huge advantage, however when it comes to root cause investigations teams do four negative and unproductive things;

(a) Teams require managing and managers will want a palatable result to report to their superiors, a result that won't harm their career path. The reality could well be bad news!

(b). Large groups, teams etc. will get distracted and most likely distract the rest of the workforce, costing time and money.

(c). No one person in the team will see all the picture. It's therefore much easier for a team to miss something.

(d) In the same way adding extra QC inspections results in lower detection rates, individuals in root cause teams (and inspection teams) psychologically relax, subconsciously thinking others will catch the issue?

Let me say again, a group/team is not how to find a root cause.

Would you want a team to drive your taxi? Pilot a plane or cross your child over the road?

If you're the boss setting up a root cause investigation, find an independent, open-minded individual who knows the process. Give him or her the problem the access to the full process, empower them with this method, and they will find the true root cause so that you're guaranteed it will never happen again.

Step 3

Access all areas

The type of process that has the issue doesn't matter. It can be anything; a financial process, a manufacturing process, a marketing process or an issue in your home life.

What a successful root cause investigation requires is full access. The investigator has to be able to begin the investigation at the very start of the process, and then to be able to follow the process all the way through to its very end. No matter where the process goes.

The reason the person, that's doing the investigating, needs to be given access to all areas is simple. They have to be able to follow the whole process, start to finish, regardless of what the processes are and where it starts and finishes.

We are talking about both physical places and digital places, the root cause investigator needs full access to the entire process.

Note: In modern businesses, chances are they will need a combination of physical and digital accesses.

Step 4

How to follow a process

Ah! I hear you say my process is office-based, I can walk it using my PC/laptop. You can, but you should also go and follow the process physically.

(If it's totally digital, then try sitting in a different office/space.)

here is what you do:

You walk methodically along the process. Consider it to be a stream, find the spring, where the process begins its life and follow it as it flows downstream.

In a business, start with the order/PO or even the tender. (Check that what you're supplying is what's on the purchase order and not what you both think you agreed on or what your company had interpreted that the customer wants. I know it sounds far-fetched, but it happens)!

As you follow the process, what you are looking for is where the process has variation, or where it doesn't follow the expected path. Ask open questions of anybody involved in the process to build up a picture of the process, and its standard deviation. It can be anyone at all, the people who work on the process are your best source as they have the expert, inside knowledge of their section of the process.

Follow the process all the way through to its end. (the customers use).

As you follow the process, do not start writing/typing/dictating detail down, the more notes you make, the more you'll get lost and miss the important things. Let me say that again, the more notes you make, the more you'll get lost.

You're there to follow the process, not to make notes. If you're checking the process against written instructions, and you notice the instructions are incorrect or missing. At this stage, it's not necessary, do not worry, just make a very short note that they need creating/changing and then continue following the process.

When I say follow the process I mean get off your butt and go and look, touch, feel, smell, listen.

Physically follow it. You've heard the saying "Walk the talk." Well, here you need to WALK THE PROCESS.

Make sure you look several times at each section.

Why numerous times? Because the root cause may be found in the different ways shifts operate, or it may be found in outside influences such as the weather or temperature differences, in procured product etc.

What you are looking for, as you follow the process is; variation, abnormalities or the unexpected, regardless of what it is.

Use your intuition and sixth sense, if you feel something isn't quiet right check it out, view it, listen to it, measure it, smell and if it's a food process and safe, taste it. As you go, keep asking questions. (Don't stop when you reach the point where the issue was found, work from the start to the very end).

The reason for this beginning to end investigation is that where you may think/guess/feel the problem is, quite likely is not where it originated. In other words, where the root cause really is, may be much earlier in the process, or it may even be after where the issue becomes apparent.

Step 5

Using comparators

If you are lucky enough to have a comparator, check the process against that.

You can also use a step back in time as a comparator when the process was working OK.

It might be there is absolutely no data for this process, or it might be you have a mass of data, what you want to do at this stage is just store it as you go. Don't worry if there is zero data at this stage. When you discover data, simply put it in a file or place a link to it into a file for later analysis.

If you're lucky, you will have a comparator, by this we mean a very similar process or a second shift/line to compare the faulty process with.

When using a comparator, what you're looking for is differences. No matter what the differences are, check them out.

Don't try to change the world when you find a difference. Just satisfy yourself of two things;

(a). Is the difference causing non conformance and

(b). Is this difference causing the issue?

A word of warning—when you find a difference, DO NOT get it changed/adjusted or fixed. In fact, if you possibly can, don't tell anyone for now.

I can hear you saying; Why not get it put right, after all, that's what we are here for!

Yes, and we will be able to correct it, but let's do it when we've found the far more important root cause. If we fix it now, we risk masking and hiding the thing we are looking for. So look at the bigger picture and unless it's a health and safety risk, park it temporary until you've found the root cause.

In the same way when you find errors in written documentation make a brief note, so it's not forgotten later and then move on.

To reiterate, when you are lucky enough to have the same (please note I'm not using the word identical), processes try to spot what and where the differences are between the two processes. At this stage, you're only doing one thing. Observing. It's an overview you need to get, NOT to get bogged down in detail at any stage. Use your instincts when following the process and do not ask for data at this stage.

A quick point about working on the shop floor and getting the best from the production team. In the same way as children can smell a student teacher a mile off! From a practical perspective, don't turn up with a Saville row suit or start ordering people about. Let them guide you in what to wear and how to talk. Let them do their job and try your best to fit in with them.

You cannot dispense with their experience and cooperation, so try to be friendly.

If you're a sole trader you're still going to need the cooperation of your suppliers, customers, and people who work in a similar type of work to yourself.

If it's an office-based process you're looking at, dress in the same manner as the rest of the office staff do.

If you're on the shop floor. Dump the suit and tie, look at what the staff in that area normally wear, if it's normally jeans and a T-shirt. Wear the same if you don't already.

The reason for this is; you're already going to stand out like a sore thumb and stop people doing things in a normal, natural way. So, as we've already said, follow the area's dress code. In addition, be mindful and try to stand where you can view what you need to see, but where you're NOT in the way of the operation. Be aware that the shift/department may have already swapped out the usual person for the supervisor or the most experienced person in that area to do the operation. Why? Because they are worried about what you'll see! So, the next day or a week later when they are not expecting you, go and watch it again and again until they are used to you being around. (This is another reason why you should only report small, minor issues at the end of your investigation. Otherwise, you'll lose all of your coworkers/staff's confidence and good will). The only exception is, if there is a health and safety issue to what you've found. If this is the case, report it immediately.

Try your best to let them do their job/role/part in the normal, natural way.

What if you've followed the process, and you've not found anything?

Foremost, you need to understand you can't hit the jackpot first time, every time. In fact, it's rare to find the root cause immediately.

So if you've followed all the process and nothing has jumped out at you, or you suspect a part of the process but can't quiet work out what's going on, don't worry.

Just do a quick sanity check, by double-checking you've followed the whole process from the very beginning to the very end. Making a process flow diagram might help to show if you've missed anything.

At this point, you may have a good feeling about what's happening, or you may have zero. Either way, let's move to the next step.

Step 6

Data

Data collection

Let's start by debunking a general routine that too many people jump head first into when given a root cause to work on. That is collecting as much data and documentation as they possibly can, even if it has the most tenuous link to the subject. Often this is done in the mistaken belief, the answer is in there somewhere and this shows how busy they've been. i.e., there is a need to instantly to have something to show for their time and effort. This mistake can be compounded by bosses who also don't know what they're doing, when it comes to finding a root cause. The boss sees his/her staff running around collecting data and documents. This makes the boss think that they are all being great workers and doing a really top job.

Let me tell you how this pans out when you've got somebody doing the root cause investigation that really doesn't know what the hell they are doing. The boss gave them this task, so they get on with it, (when there is probably somebody else in the department that is better suited). The pressure is on to look like they know what they're doing and to look busy. So, they set off at 100 miles an hour, opening files and starting databases, doing anything to look like they're working really hard. In reality, what they are doing is an awful lot of meaningless work. Or worse still muddling the water.

The reason I'm explaining this is so that you'll hopefully be able to spot yourself going down this route and turn yourself around, or you'll see it in others and be able to help them.

What happens next is the instance they find, in all this confusion of data and documentation, a small error, an incorrect reference or a work instruction that hasn't been updated. Or some such item with a small error, they dive on it and make a fuss about getting it corrected.

What this type of unstructured work is really doing is housekeeping and polishing, it's not fixing anything important. They are going off at a busy looking tangent. Which will ultimately lead them straight down a housekeeping rabbit hole.

It's a simple mistake that we've all made in one way or another at home and at work. Happily fixing little unimportant things. Thinking we're doing well as we are busy, BUT in reality none of this is resolving the problem.

We need to look at the big picture, not the detail. (Refer to the issue description in your notebook).

Time is always ticking and running away, the customer is still getting poor product/service. The business is still wasting money and certainly is not being efficient.

It gets worse because the initial problem/issue/disaster gets forgotten and left behind as more and more people get involved busily resolving minor issues that have probably been there for years, issues the product has happily passed by, while finishing in a conforming state.

All that this activity achieves is polishing. It's a nice to have, not a must-have!

You must keep your eye on the target, (the issue we wrote down in our pocket notebook); otherwise the root cause investigation will get lost and forgotten, hidden behind the 'nice to have's' that make no/little difference to the product.

Too much data also means too much time and effort trying to sort and filter it all.

This really is a danger. Allow me to explain to you why, there is a danger in too much data and especially in non-subject specific data.

The danger is, you'll find yourself trying to sort through terabytes of data instead of looking at the problem and attempting to find the answer.

There is a time frame in which you have to find the root cause. If you're a sole trader, you can't spend forever on it, as you still need to run your business. If you're in a big company, the boss will run out of patience at some point. So, regardless of what the size of your organization, it's important to focus your efforts and not to waste time on irrelevant data and detail.

Let's be clear, there is no doubt the answer can be found in the data. It can be found through tools like SPC (statistical process control), CMM (Coordinate Measuring Machines) reports and accounting figures. In your particular circumstances, you will know which tool or techniques will give you the best results, but please do not just start shifting through mountains of data. Be specific and only look at data related to the issue. There is a saying "The more data the better" but when it comes to root cause too much data will be a distraction danger, where you risk getting lost in it. You just need to have a minimum amount of data to give you evidence. You can always add to it later to give strength to your case or as a sanity check to confirm your findings.

A simple way to limit the data is to pick a specific time frame. Pick a point where things were going to plan (producing conforming product/service) and a second point not long after where things were going wrong.

Limit yourself initially to this period to reduce the time and effort needed to check through the data.

Another simple way to limit your time and effort is to stick to the part number or account number to begin with. If you don't see trends or patterns in the data, then you can incrementally expand your search until, hopefully, you do so.

At this stage if you find something, don't do anything with the information you find in the data, (obviously humans and especially engineers are preprogrammed to find a solution and mend anything and everything that's not working correctly). You need to suppress that natural feeling until you've double-checked and until you've found the root cause.

The data may well be showing you an effect or cause but not the root cause! (See chapter 3).

Double-check your findings, then use the information to find the root cause.(see chapter 5).

As we mentioned earlier, the reason you shouldn't say anything at this point, instead complete your checks and complete your investigation. Try to write up your findings before anyone changes things. (The only exception is, if there is a health and safety issue).

Step 7

Time to make a change

You can use this step if you still haven't found the root cause or if you want to confirm what you have already found. In fact, it can also be used to prove to a wider audience that you really have found the true root cause. (This will be especially useful if previously others have tried in vain to resolve this problem. These are the people who will be shocked you've done what they failed to do. So, they are going to take a little extra convincing).

WARNING

Just a word of warning before we begin. It's hoped you've found the root cause before this point because you need to be careful any change you make are within the process's tolerance.

i.e., unless your process makes cheap low-cost product, where it's okay (using cost benefit analysis), to scrap a few products to find out what's going on. Alternatively, if you can run a trial that will never get to the customer.

That said, let's look at this step in detail.

In this step, we change something to see how it affects the results. If you have a nagging suspicion, you can start at that part of the process.

If you still have no clue or only a little hunch, start at the END of the process and work backwards.

Why start at the end and not at the beginning?

Because starting at the end, you'll only be impacting one step (the last one), instead of all of them. To put it another way, if you change something at the beginning, the ripple effect could change many things further along the process, giving strange and weird results. This is likely to mask any findings you have and confuse the good work you've done so far. In short, it will be difficult/impossible to interpret the results. Whereas, if you start at the END, you'll easily see what is happening and gain an insight into the process. An insight few or no one will have been privileged too before.

What you do is; on the section of the process you have a hunch on or on the last section of the process, (if you have no Scooby instincts) is to swap something over in that area.

Let's look at a couple of examples:

Example 1

Let's say the end of your process is a CMM inspection operation. Then use a different department's CMM and operators. (If you only have the one CMM on site, then send the product out to an independent inspection house and get a CMM report from them).

Example 2

Let's say the operation you have is the spray-painting process. In this case, swapping out the sprayer and his spray gun may not be practical, they may be the company's only one. So see if you can loan one from somewhere, an adjacent business, a hire shop or send the product to another company for them to paint.

Example 3

An office-based accounting process.

Let's say the final part of the process is to email the final audited figures to your customers.

Try getting figures audited by a different person and the email process changed from a manual process to an automated one.

If, swapped out, shows no changes, you have at least learned something (chances are the root cause isn't in that area and that part of the process isn't sensitive to it). Work backwards, eliminating section by section. Only make a quick note, or you can just mentally remember it's not this part of the process. Keep moving back through the process until you find something. Assess it, if it's not the root cause, keep going.

If it's still not jumped out at you even though you've been thorough and even double-checked everything, then what?

ELIMINATION

As Sherlock Homes said, "Once you have eliminated all other possibilities, what you're left with is the answer."

So, we start working through the process eliminating one part of the process and then the next,

in this way you should end up with one or two sections of the process.

Why did we not start with this method? Because to do this elimination, you need to be, what you have now become, an experienced expert in this process.

Once you find the issue's source, dig right down to the true root cause. Always do the 5Y's (Five why's).

The five whys will check your work, if you're now confident you know what the root cause is.

Chapter 5

5Ys

5Y's or five why's.

5Y's or five whys.

Let's be clear about this, 5Y's (five whys) is the only root cause method that works outside a theory book or a classroom.

That said, 5Y's will only work in conjunction with an investigation.

For those of you new to 5Y's (five whys) I'll give you a simple explanation, but like most things in life, practice makes perfect. So if you're new to it, try using 5Y's on a few scenarios of your own, (real or imaginary) before you put the world right on your first attempt.

5Ys

Always begin by going back to your original description in your root cause notebook (or wherever you originally wrote it down). Find the original problem/issue/disaster definition and copy it word for word.

Your 5Y begins in the right direction by using that original definition.

For example, if your original definition read: The train jumped the tracks and crashed.

Then you would begin your 5Y's by writing down;

WHY did The train jump the tracks and crash?

Because you will have carried out a full root cause investigation, you will now be able to confidently answer this question, using what the investigation taught you.

So after this first Why question, comes your answer. Which will be based on a cause, NOT an effect.

In this example, the answer would look like this;

Because the train was traveling too fast.

The answer to the first Why will now become the text to your second Why.

In this way, we keep a progression going from one question to the next. Each question drilling down to the root. (Not keeping this progression is where most 5Y's go wrong). Your root cause must keep drilling down one step and one WHY at a time.

The second WHY question would now read,

WHY was the train traveling too fast?

5Y's is so named because most of the time before you get to the fifth, WHY? You should have reached the root cause.

It can be less than five WHY questions, and it can be more. (Don't worry if you go over five Y's, just double-check you're not going off at a tangent).

How do I know when I've asked enough WHY questions?

Experience, of course, will be a big help, but in most cases you'll reach an answer similar to the previous answer or the answer will be a fact.

Here are three examples.

5Y's example 1

Let's start with Fred's bike again because by now you'll know his puncture process very well.

ISSUE: The tire has a puncture.

(1) WHY has the tire got a puncture?

ANSWER: Because the inner tube has a hole in it.

(2nd) WHY has the inner tube has a hole in it?

ANSWER: A thorn has gone through the tire into the inner tube.

(3rd) WHY has a thorn gone through the tire into the inner tube?

ANSWER: Fred rides his bike down a lane where he knows the hawthorn hedge is regularly cut.

(4th) WHY did Fred ride his bike down a lane where he knows the hawthorn hedge is regularly cut.

ANSWER: Because it's a shortcut home at the end of each week's ride.

If we asked a fifth WHY question, the answer would be similar to because he did! So, we have reached a point where the root cause lies.

Therefore, the root cause of Fred's puncture is;

Fred takes a shortcut home.

It's important to define how to correct the root cause, we will discuss this further in the next chapter, but for now, let's stick to this issue.

Corrective action; Fred stops using the shortcut and rides home, at the end of each Saturday's ride, on regular roads.

5Ys, example number two.

In this second scenario, we have a business whose product is high-end solid hardwood doors. Their issue is that on irregular occasions during the computer controlled routing process, the hard wood splinters and ruin's the door's finish.

The business needs to know what the root cause is so that they can prevent the splintering happening in the future,

As with all root cause investigations before the 5 why's you absolutely have to complete the investigation first.

Let's say the investigation was completed and the cause of splintering during the machining of hardwood doors was found to be blunt routing cutters.

The reason you have to complete the investigation first is because the 5 why's is totally useless without it. There is an elementary reason behind the need for an investigation. Without it there is no direction to the 5y they go together. Investigation First, then the 5 why's. They go hand-in-hand. Investigation first, then the five why's.

The investigation no matter how thorough and complete doesn't drill down far enough, that's where the 5 why's comes in.

Without the investigation, the 5 why has no direction, and it is just a stab in the dark.

Let's repeat investigation first, 5 why's second.

As we discussed always start the five whys with the original problem definition. The one that's written in your notebook. The definition that guided you throughout your investigation.

First WHY; Why, during the computer controlled routing process, does the hard wood splinter and ruin the door's finish.

Answer; Splintering during the machining of hardwood door panels was found to be caused by blunt cutters.

Second, WHY; Why are blunt cutters being used in the routing process?

Answer; At times blunt cutters are being used because there is no tool life testing or tool control process.

Third WHY; Why is there no tool control/tool life process in place.

Answer; Because the business didn't have time as it was fulfilling orders.

Fourth, WHY; Why didn't the business find time to implement a tool life/tool control process.

Answer; Because it was a business decision made by the management at the time.

If we ask any further why, we'll just keep going around in circles because it was a decision that was made at the time. (If we ask another why, the answer will be because it was). Therefore, we have reached the root cause.

The root cause is, it was a management decision made at the time. (Possibly because the business was immature and meeting orders, at the time, used 100% of their resource).

When you create your report/ presentation you need to put in all the things you've learned from your investigation, and importantly you also have to put at the end of the presentation a corrective action.

Why do you have to put in a corrective action? Because you are now the process expert. The company/ manager may decide to implement an entirely different corrective action to the one you suggest!

This may cause the original issue to come back again. If you don't propose a corrective action and the issue comes back due to a misguided/mad manager, it will look awful on you. However, if you document the corrective action and then the business /mad manager decide to put in a different corrective action, (that doesn't work) in place. It will look terrible on them.

So always include the corrective action in your root cause presentation.

Third 5Ys example

In this scenario we are going to look at an issue with a digital documentation process.

The business's issue is; they have put numerous tenders forward for work and haven't secured a single successful work package.

The investigation was carried out and established that tenders submitted in the previous month's have been lacking detail, in particular how the business proposed to meet the contract's demanding specifications.

The lack of detail was found to be due to a heavy workload (of many tenders), over a short time frame. Key members of staff were off, on long-term sick leave. To compound the problem, over this period there were more tenders than normal.

The investigation has been completed and done its work. Now let's use the five why's to drill down to the true root cause.

First WHY; Why has the large number of tenders submitted, not secured a single work package?

Answer; Tenders have been lacking detail, in particular how the business proposed to meet the contract's demanding specifications.

2nd, WHY; why did the tenders lack specific detail.

Answer; The lack of specific detail was due to an imbalance in the staff/workload ratio.

Third, WHY;; Why was there an imbalance in the staff/workload ratio.

Answer; because there wasn't enough experienced staff and extra tenders.

Fourth WHY; Why wasn't there enough experienced staff.

Answer; because the engineer who normally writes the specifications is off work with a long-term illness.

Fifth, WHY; Why wasn't additional staff drafted into help?

Answer The directors didn't want the additional cost.

Now we have a root cause; that the directors didn't want an additional cost.

At the time, the directors didn't see that the business wouldn't get zero return from the tenders!

'Penny wise, pound foolish' is an apt saying in this case.

What would be a corrective action for this example; Well, going forward the business would be wise to generate a plan to mitigate when a minimum number of staff are working on tenders.

The plan would include such things as drafting in staff from another part of the business, concentrating on fully completing the more profitable tenders and hiring in contract staff.

A documented lessons learned should also be part of the corrective action.

In all the examples, it's important to remember. It's investigation first, 5Y's second.

Chapter 6

Present your findings and define corrective action

Take time to write your root cause presentation/report because unlike most reports, root cause presentations will have a company-wide audience. So ensure that your findings can be communicated across the companies range of communication skills. Use photos where you can.

If your company has a non conformance system, don't forget to complete your tasks in it.

It's important to include evidence in your presentation along with your findings.

Ensure your presentation/report details corrective actions.

Why include corrective action in your root cause presentation? Because you are now the process expert. The company/manager may decide to implement an entirely different corrective action to the one you know is correct!

A different corrective action may cause the original issue to come back again. If you don't recommend a corrective action and the issue comes back due to a misguided manager, it will look awful on you. However, if you document the corrective action and then the business/manager decide to put in a different corrective action, (that doesn't work) it will look terrible on them. So add your corrective action to your report to protect yourself.

Finally, include a documented lesson learned so that your findings can be referred back to at a later date.

And last but not lease, thank all the people who helped you.

Note: now is the time to go through your notebook and report all the small issues you found during your investigation.

The end

If you enjoyed this book please tell others about it.

Leaving positive feedback really helps.

Thanks

Other titles by the same author

Children's books by **Dave B**

What would you like

A day out at the sea

The new bat

A day at the zoo

Hi

Children's books in French by **Dave B**

Que désirez-vous

Young adult's fiction books by **Dave B**

What if

Young adult's fiction books in French by **Dave B**

Et qu'est-ce qui se passerait si

Adult fiction books BY **DAVE BUXTON**

YOUR OBITUARY

Keepnet

<u>Information books</u> by **DAVID BUXTON**

How to have a good night's sleep with your baby

www.ingramcontent.com/pod-product-compliance
Lightning Source LLC
Chambersburg PA
CBHW031433250726